THE
OTTER TRAIL

*To my parents, Nigel and Truida,
with love*

THE OTTER TRAIL

and the
Tsitsikamma Coastal
National Park

PATRICK WAGNER

STRUIK PUBLISHERS

STRUIK PUBLISHERS (PTY) LTD
(A MEMBER OF THE STRUIK
PUBLISHING GROUP (PTY) LTD
CORNELIS STRUIK HOUSE
80 MCKENZIE STREET
CAPE TOWN 8001

REG. NO.: 54/00965/07

TEXT © PATRICK WAGNER
PHOTOGRAPHS © PATRICK WAGNER,
AND INDIVIDUAL PHOTOGRAPHERS
LISTED IN ACKNOWLEDGEMENTS ON
PAGE 48.

EDITOR: KATE MCCALLUM
DESIGN AND TYPOGRAPHY:
WIM REINDERS & ASSOCIATES
COVER DESIGN: NEVILLE POULTER

TYPESETTING BY MCMANUS BROS
REPRODUCTION BY UNIFOTO
(PTY) LTD, CAPE TOWN
PRINTING AND BINDING BY KYODO
PRINTING CO (SINGAPORE) PTE LTD

FIRST PUBLISHED 1988
SECOND IMPRESSION 1991
SECOND EDITION 1993
SECOND IMPRESSION 1996

ISBN 1 86825 339 2

Front cover: *The Bloukrans River,
crossed on the fourth day of the Otter
Trail, is one of the highlights of the trail.*
Page 1: *Much of the Otter Trail runs
close to the sea, providing hikers with
spectacular views.*
Pages 2-3: *The last two days of the
Otter Trail take the hiker along the top
of towering cliffs and through coastal
fynbos.*
Above: *Calm conditions such as these
are a rare feature of the aptly named
Storms River Mouth.*

CONTENTS

THE TSITSIKAMMA COASTAL
NATIONAL PARK:
TRAILS AND FACILITIES   6
THE MOUTH TRAIL   8
STORMS RIVER ADVENTURE   9
THE LOERIE TRAIL   9
THE BLUE DUIKER TRAIL   9
THE WATERFALL TRAIL   9
ANGLING   10
THE UNDERWATER TRAIL   10
THE SCUBA TRAIL   11

THE ECOSYSTEM OF
THE INDIGENOUS FOREST   12

THE OTTER TRAIL   18
DAY ONE   20
DAY TWO   24
DAY THREE   32
DAY FOUR   38
DAY FIVE   44

USEFUL INFORMATION   48

*The power of the sea is revealed in a
dramatic seascape at Skietklip.*

THE TSITSIKAMMA
COASTAL NATIONAL PARK

*Trails
and
facilities*

Along the shores of one of the most dangerous coastlines in the world – the southern Cape coastline – a coastal national park maintains its existence.

The Tsitsikamma Coastal National Park extends from the Groot River in Nature's Valley to another river similarly called the Groot River, near the resort Eersterivier. Between these two borders lie eighty kilometres of beautiful indigenous forest and fynbos vegetation. Being a coastal park, it stretches a mere half kilometre inland and five kilometres out to sea, thus creating a well-defined marine reserve.

This area of unique beauty has a considerable amount of activity available to the outdoor enthusiast. The Park is roughly bisected in two by the precipitous Storms River gorge. Where this river enters the sea, the Park headquarters and restcamp nestle among the towering cliffs and indigenous forest vegetation.

The area to the east of the restcamp, from the Storms River to Eersterivier, is a restricted area, limited to Parks Board personnel only. The area to the west of the restcamp, from Storms River to Nature's Valley, is the famous Otter Trail, about forty-five kilometres of true outdoor hiking spirit.

The number of vehicles per day in the Park is limited, as the area is a national park, and the fauna and flora would not be able to handle a disproportionate number of visitors. The human impact on a nature reserve can be devastating, so to avoid any deterioration of natural assets, the number of people entering daily has to be limited.

After paying a small entrance fee at the gate the visitor winds down the pass through the forest to the restcamp area. The restaurant at Storms River Mouth has one of the most rewarding views of any restaurant in South Africa. The windows open out onto the blue seas of the Indian Ocean, the green shades of the indigenous forest and the black geometry of the surrounding vertical geological structure of Table Mountain sandstone.

Overnight accommodation is also available to the visitor. Basic campsites for tents and caravans are available at a nominal rate, but for those who seek

Left: *The suspension bridge crossing the Storms River is an endless source of delight to walkers along the Mouth Trail.*
Right: *A detour along the Mouth Trail reveals Kerneels se Klip, one of the many fascinating rock formations in this area.*

Above, left: *One of nature's most powerful weathering tools, the sea continually shapes and sculpts the coastal rocks.*

Above, right: *In poor weather the Storms River lives up to its name and reputation.*

Opposite page: *The Black oystercatcher* (Haematopus moquini) *is an unmistakable resident of the Tsitsikamma shoreline.*

a greater degree of comfort, beach cottages, chalets and the "oceanettes" provide an excellent venue for relaxation.

All tourist activity is confined to the restcamp area, and the Otter Trail section of the Park is open only to those who have booked to do the trail. Any other section of the Park is closed to the general public. However, there are a number of short trails in the restcamp area.

The Mouth Trail is perhaps the most popular of the four short trails. Extending from the restaurant to the mouth of the Storms River this trail winds through the forest for about one kilometre and then spans the beautiful steep gorge of the Storms River by means of a suspension bridge. According to visitors, the bridge is the greatest attraction of the trail.

The Mouth Trail has several attractive diversions en route to the bridge. Mooibaai is a neat little cove tucked away into the forest, providing an excellent swimming and sunbathing venue when sea conditions allow.

After the turn-off to Mooibaai there is a very basic open-air "museum" supplying information on tree identification, the forest structure and the ecosystem. Rough wooden display cabinets contain artists' impressions and diagrams.

The turn-off to Driftwood Bay is found at the open-air museum. Driftwood Bay is a rocky beach littered with masses of uniquely designed, attractive forms of wood which have been sculptured by the elements. Although an obvious temptation to souvenir hunters, the driftwood may not be removed as the area is within a national park, where no plant, object or animal of any description whatsoever may be disturbed or removed.

The next turn-off winds down to a small uniquely sculptured bay containing an interesting prominent rock design – hence its name, Kerneels se Klip. Kerneels se Klip is a small isolated area that offers an encompassing feeling of solitude for those who want to be alone for a while.

On the western bank of the Storms River gorge, the Strandloper Cave is easily accessible. The coastline is riddled with caves that were once inhabited by the Khoi-Khoi. It is from these people that the name "Tsitsikamma" comes. "Tsitsikamma" is the Khoi-Khoi word for falling water, clear water and the sound of rain. We will never know the exact meaning because we have never heard the old language being spoken. The name does, however, describe very accurately the climate of the area – a high rainfall region receiving 1 200 mm per annum.

After crossing the Storms River by means of the suspension bridge, the trail to the lookout point winds up a small nearby gorge.

For the very adventurous *the Storms River* offers yet another wonderful experience. A trip down the river on tubes never ceases to be a delight. This journey can be extremely dangerous, so you should be well prepared, and plan the trip carefully. Before attempting the journey permission must be obtained from the Department of Forestry and the National Parks Board, because the land being crossed falls under their jurisdiction. While obtaining the necessary permits from these people, enquire about the dangers involved and plan your journey according to their advice.

The Loerie Trail is a short trail – one kilometre in length – which winds through the forest close to the restcamp. The atmosphere on the trail is breathtaking, as the route bridges a few small rivers offering a peaceful delight, and the muffled crashing of the waves becomes fainter as you venture deeper into the forest. This is an ideal place for keen birdwatchers, as the forest supports a wide diversity of bird species. The trail is named after one of these birds – the Knysna Loerie – an extremely attractive fruit-eating bird that lives in the forest canopy.

The Blue Duiker Trail offers scenery similar to that of the Loerie Trail. Slightly longer than the Loerie Trail – three kilometres in length – it leads deeper into the forest and should rather be tackled by the more adventurous.

The blue duiker is a small shy forest antelope, and a few fortunate visitors might encounter this little animal on the trail. As forest animals are very shy and timid, any visitor wishing to see wildlife should walk quietly in the early morning and late evening, for it is during these hours that the animals are most active.

The Waterfall Trail is in fact the first three kilometres of the Otter Trail. Beginning at the official starting point of the Otter Trail – a cairn of stones next to the parking bays at the oceanettes – the trail leads in a westerly direction towards Nature's Valley. Here the walker is given a small taste of the beauty that the Otter Trail offers. No hikers other than the official Otter Trail hikers may venture beyond the waterfall, so at this point the general visitor will have to follow the same trail back to the oceanettes.

Anglers will be happy to know that their needs have been seen to. The Waterfall Trail and the coast directly in front of the oceanettes is open to rock angling. As the area is a national park no bait or any marine organisms may be removed from the rocks. Fortunately the shop at the restcamp solves a possible bait-shortage by supplying bait to the public. The Tsitsikamma area has a rich supply of fish and some of the best rock angling facilities in the country. This three-kilometre stretch of coastline is the only section of the Park that is open for angling.

The Storms River Mouth near the restcamp area can produce some wonderful places for swimming and diving. Being one of the most dangerous coastlines in the world the area lives up to its name of the Storms River. However, when sea conditions allow the area can be a paradise for bathers and divers.

The Park boasts the only *underwater trail* in the country. In order to maintain an accident-free underwater trail there are hard and fast rules and regulations. During the season, Parks Board personnel provide guided trails. This includes the hiking trails and the underwater trails. Guided hiking trails are relatively accident-free so very few rules are invoked during the trails. The Underwater Trail is a different story altogether. Snorkel divers may dive at any time, providing they supply their own equipment. During guided snorkel trails only basic snorkel equipment is issued to visitors free of charge for the duration of the trail.

For *the Scuba Trail*, divers must be able to produce a two-star or equivalent diving qualification recognised by the South African Underwater Union. One-star divers may dive if they are accompanied by a two-star diver. Divers must provide all their own scuba diving gear, as the Parks Board will not hire or lend out any scuba equipment. (Divers should note that there is no air facility in the Park, the closest facility being the Beacon Isle Hotel at Plettenberg Bay.)

Opposite page: *This calm river overhung by ferns and forest trees is crossed by the Loerie Trail.*
Left: *Deeper into the forest, a tranquil waterfall and river form part of the scenery on the Blue Duiker Trail.*
Right: *The characteristically flaky bark of the Outeniqua Yellowwood* (Podocarpus falcatus) *is apparent on this trunk.*

11

THE ECOSYSTEM OF
THE INDIGENOUS FOREST

The concept of what comprises an indigenous forest is completely misunderstood by many. It is believed to be a vastly rich and fertile ecosystem that supports most forms of flora and fauna. However, it is an area in which an extremely delicate balance is maintained – which would be easily upset through careless use or management. In order to appreciate the beauty and some of the rules associated with the Otter Trail, perhaps it would be wise to understand just how the forest ecosystem functions.

For the sake of simplicity, the forest can be divided into various horizontal layers or strata. The uppermost layer or tree canopy supports a food web which experiences elements unknown to the forest floor – full exposure to the sun and wind. Hot "berg" winds cause accelerated evaporation from the surface of the leaves, so to survive the leaves of the upper canopy have become reduced in size and generally small. Along the coastal areas some of the trees have evolved a waxy surface layer or cuticle as a protective mechanism against the damaging effect of wind-borne salt spray.

Candlewood (*Pterocelastrus tricuspidatus*) and Milkwood (*Sideroxylon inerme*) are two of the dominant coastal trees that have developed waxy leaves. Other common trees include Red Saffron (*Cassine crocea*), Bastard Saffron (*Cassine peragua*), Red Currant (*Rhus chirindensis*) and Camphor Bush (*Tarchonanthus camphoratus*).

Directly on the coastline the horizontal structure of the forest is less well defined. Moving inland away from the immediate coastline, strata become more apparent and the dominant species change. Here one encounters Hard Pear (*Olinia ventosa*), White Pear (*Apodytes dimidiata*), Real Yellowwood (*Podocarpus latifolius*), Cape Beech (*Rapanea melanophloeos*), Bastard Ironwood (*Olea capensis*), Forest Elder (*Nuxia floribunda*) and Cape Ash (*Ekebergia capensis*).

Flowers produced by the upper canopy trees attract insects and birds for pollination and later develop into fruits. These fruits are then consumed by birds and monkeys and the seeds voided, in this way dispersing the seed. At

Left: *A Stinkwood tree* (Ocotea bullata) *points vertically towards the forest canopy.*
Right: *The Knysna Loerie* (Tauraco corythaix) *tends to be difficult to photograph because it lives high in the forest canopy.*

13

night the process continues with moths, fruit- and insect-eating bats venturing into the darkness when there is less competition from other animals.

Lower down, about ten to fifteen metres off the ground, the trees making up the lower canopy are encountered. These include Kamassi (*Gonioma kamassi*), Assegai (*Curtisia dentata*) and Cape Blackwood (*Maytenus peduncularis*) and are usually small to medium-sized individuals which rarely attain upper canopy status.

Lianas, more commonly known as monkey ropes, are twisted around the branches of both the upper and lower canopies and have a dual function. They help support the tall tree trunks and also serve as routes of convenience, joining the canopies above and the forest floor below.

A layer of bush extends three to five metres above the forest floor and is composed mainly of thorny scramblers such as the the Num Num bush (*Carissa bispinosa*) and Common Spikethorn (*Maytenus heterophylla*) and a rather hairy species, the Witchhazel (*Trichocladus crinitus*). These two characteristics – the possession of hairy leaves and the presence of sharp thorns – render them unpalatable and thus reduces the probability of their being browsed.

Where tree meets soil, a few interesting features become apparent. Tall trunks, developing strong flutings and plank buttresses at maturity (as in *Ocotea bullata*, for example), are supported by buttress roots, an important feature in view of the shallow root system of most forest species. One advantage of having a shallow root system is that this enables them to take up essential nutrients and moisture present in the ground litter layer. This litter layer is composed of dead and decaying organic matter which is constantly replaced from the trees above. It forms the first link in the food chain upon which man is ultimately dependent.

The important role which the litter layer plays in the forest ecosystem is evident if one looks at a few of its functions. Not only does it provide a source of nutrients for plant growth and development, but it also conserves soil moisture by reducing evaporation. Water run-off is retarded by the thick litter layer, thus reducing erosion and promoting water retention. Suitable microhabitats are created for seed germination and organisms responsible for the breakdown of litter find shelter and food within this layer.

Bacteria, moulds and fungi are the first agents of degradation. Fungal threads form a network, or mycelium, which pervades the litter, producing enzymes capable of breaking it down into smaller components which then act as a food source.

The ground litter layer is composed not only of leaf litter but also of larger plant debris such as dead tree trunks resulting from the death of a tree through old age, and fallen branch wood produced by strong winds.

Unlike most creatures, which are unable to digest the woody component of ground litter, termites and wood-boring beetles possess protozoa and bacteria in their digestive tracts which are capable of breaking down wood fibres, lignin and cellulose. The termites and beetles are in turn preyed upon by other insects, frogs, birds and small mammals and in this way reintroduce nutrients into the food chain.

A feature which you will almost certainly become aware of as you make your way along the trail, is that water flowing in the streams and rivers is brown in colour. This strange coloration is due to the presence of tannins, which are picked up by the water as it percolates through the organic litter layer. The presence of this brown pigment is perfectly harmless and the river water is quite acceptable for drinking.

In summary, the ground litter layer is most important as a source of nutrients, a means of water conservation and as a refuge for decomposer organisms which form a vital link in forest food chains and nutrient cycles. In the Tsitsikamma forest this organic layer is thin, a mere one metre thick in places, and, once removed, takes many years, perhaps even centuries, to

replace. It therefore becomes clear that a high concentration of hikers on a single trail can cause irreversible problems. An average of 3 500 people hike the Otter Trail every year. This means that the trail has to be managed very carefully, using a sound system of rules and regulations.

Another important area of the indigenous forest is the forest edge or margin. Here, where forest meets fynbos, a distinct marginal flora is present and may form either an abrupt, well-defined edge or a less clearly defined, intergrading margin. The marginal flora has the dual function of providing a buffer against fire and of maintaining a barrier which prevents penetration of the forest and hence drying out of the forest floor. Examples of marginal flora includes the Blossom Tree (*Virgilia oroboides*) and the Bush Tick Berry (*Chrysanthemoides monilifera*).

The indigenous forest is not the only vegetation type encountered along the Otter Trail. Coastal fynbos is particularly dominant, especially on the last two days. Fynbos is an extremely complex vegetation type. It forms a low-

Opposite page: *Sunlight outlines the delicate green tracery of the leaves of the Common Star Apple* (Diospyros dichrophylla).
Left: *A hiker walks through a clearing in the indigenous forest.*
Right, above and below: *Fungi are among some of the exquisite forms and textures to be found in the indigenous forest.*

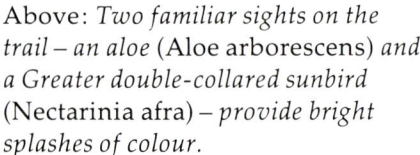

Above: *Two familiar sights on the trail – an aloe* (Aloe arborescens) *and a Greater double-collared sunbird* (Nectarinia afra) *– provide bright splashes of colour.*

Top, right: *Constructing its magnificent web design across the forest floor, a spider waits for its prey.*

Below, right: *Hardy Gazania daisies grow in a crack in a lichen-stained rock.*

lying scrub-type vegetation in places and is adapted to summer drought and nutrient-poor soils. The three most common families that constitute fynbos are the Ericaceae, Proteaceae and Restionaceae. It is particularly famous for its Protea family, the King Protea (*Protea cynaroides*) being South Africa's national flower.

The forest does contain a small variety of mammalian wildlife but, being extremely shy, these animals are very rarely seen. The forest leopard, caracal, honey badger, large spotted genet, Cape clawless otter, water mongoose, and grey mongoose are the most dominant predators in the forest. Bushpig, vervet monkey, bushbuck, blue duiker and rock hyrax are the most dominant herbivores.

Above and below: *Actually two "plants" – algae and fungi existing in a symbiotic relationship – lichen coats the rocks in a delicate array of green, orange, grey and black.*

THE OTTER TRAIL

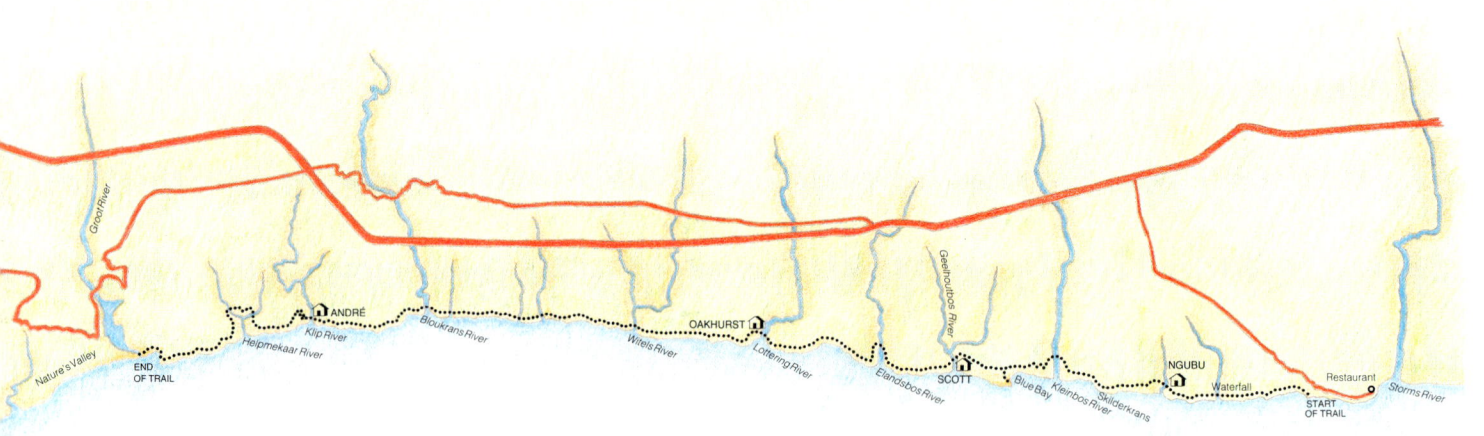

In 1964 a thin section of rugged coastline in the Tsitsikamma area was handed over to the National Parks Board after previously belonging to the Department of Forestry. This year marked the official proclamation of the Tsitsikamma Coastal National Park.

In 1965 the idea of a hiking trail along the coastline was initiated by Dr G A Robinson, the park warden at the time. After three years of dedication and hard work the Otter Hiking Trail was born in 1968.

Initially the trail could accommodate only ten people each day, as there was only one very basic hut at each overnight spot. Ten years later the trail suddenly became very popular, which led to the construction of two new huts at each overnight spot in 1985, thus increasing the daily hiking party to a maximum of twelve people only.

The first hut, Ngubu, is named after Sergeant Petrus Ngubu, a ranger at the Park who died later in a tragic accident. The second hut, Scott, is named after Popo Scott, who is still working at the Park today as one of the senior rangers.

The third hut, Oakhurst, is named after the Oakhurst Forestry Station nearby. The last hut, André, is named after André Kok, the restcamp manager at the time.

The Otter Trail has been labelled as a very easy trail. For the fit, experienced hiker, the trail will prove to be easy. For those who are unfit and inexperienced an unpleasant experience lies in store. The trail has many steep inclines and descents, and a high degree of fitness is required.

The Tsitsikamma area has a high annual rainfall – 1 200 mm per annum. During heavy rains the rivers can come down in flood, resulting in dangerous conditions. Hikers who are unfortunate enough to run into difficulties at the rivers are advised to find shelter or return to the huts. Although hikers are expected to use their initiative, as this is part of the spirit of hiking, a good word of advice is not to do anything stupid. If the weather conditions remain adverse, the Parks Board will organise patrols to come to the assistance of hikers.

The Otter Trail is named after the Cape clawless otter, a shy creature that is active in the early hours of the morning and in the late evening. An excellent swimmer, it is at home in both fresh water and sea water. Sightings of otters are extremely rare, and granted only to a privileged few.

DAY ONE

4,6 km
(±3 hours)

The first day is relatively short. This gives you enough time to report to the reception desk and the information centre. Here, time is also available to organise some means of transport at Nature's Valley for the end of the hike. Most hikers leave a car at Nature's Valley, as the caravan park and the café at Nature's Valley have proved to be sufficiently safe parking areas. There is a railway bus, but the service is unreliable.

A special parking area at Storms River restcamp is provided for Otter Trail hikers and is very close to the starting point at the oceanettes, where a stone cairn marks the beginning of the trail.

The trail winds along the edge of the coastal forest, with the crashing waves often visible through the mat of overhanging vegetation. After almost one kilometre the trail opens out onto very rocky terrain. Orange otter silhouettes are painted onto the rocks at strategic points to mark the trail.

The first prominent landmark is the Guano Cave. This large cave cannot be missed as it stands out very clearly. In past years bird and bat guano were

collected from it. The trail goes past the front of the cave, winding up through the rocks and closely following the edge of the forest once again.

The trail again goes through rocky terrain, where there are beautiful rock formations designed and sculptured by the elements.

Following the rocky coastline hikers approach the halfway mark for the first day – the waterfall. This torrent tumbles down steep cliffs into a large pool, which is an excellent swimming spot.

During dry periods hikers should stock up with water at the waterfall, for the small stream that runs near the overnight point is often dry.

En route to Ngubu the trail is well established and closely hugs the edge of the forest, following the coastline. After a short ascent the trail drops down to the huts at the first overnight point, Ngubu, where there are two huts with watertanks and a chemical toilet. The huts are located close to the edge of the forest, a relatively short distance from the sea. A small stream trickles down a valley below the higher of the two huts.

Opposite page: *The first day of the trail passes close to the rocks, many of which are beautiful and strange formations.*
Left: *A common stop on the first day, this waterfall is one of the most beautiful landmarks of the trail.*
Right: *Rain washes organic material from the forest into the sand in a seaweed design.*

21

The huts at Ngubu nestle into the vegetation of the hillside, close to the sea.

22

DAY TWO

7,9 km
(±6 hours)

The second day begins with a steep climb to the top of Olienboomkop. The trail goes along the summit of the ridge above steep cliffs, and passes Skilderkrans, a magnificent viewpoint. At this point you can see much of the trail in both directions.

Past Skilderkrans the trail follows an even contour above the cliff-line, occasionally dropping into the forest to cross small streams.

A steep descent leads down into the Kleinbos River, a stop recommended by the author! A mere two hundred metres upstream from the trail, the river provides an excellent swimming spot. This river is one of those rivers on the Otter Trail which contains an unexplainable magic. The cold brutality of the steep rock creates an incredible contrast with the clear sheen of the water. Away from the muffled sound of the sea, the quiet natural beauty is stunning. This is one of those places where stiff and painful shoulders should be given a rest while chatting over a satisfying morning tea.

The trail winds up from Kleinbos River to the top of the ridge once again.

Tucked neatly into the indigenous forest close to the sound of crashing waves, the trail slowly winds down a gentle gradient, crossing a few small streams en route to Blue Bay.

Although the trail does not go through Blue Bay, but passes above it, you can take the turn-off to Blue Bay and follow the single path down to the beach. The turn-off to Blue Bay is indistinct but can be found just before the stiff climb to the top of the headland behind the bay. The return route is the same path.

Blue Bay is an excellent lunch stop and one of the highlights of the trail. The bay has wonderful contrasts of dark green forest, creamy white beach, gun-metal black rocks and deep blue green waters of the sea. When sea conditions allow, Blue Bay can be a wonderful swimming spot, very often providing the more enthusiastic hiker with an exciting taste of bodysurfing.

Feeling rested and recharged, you can follow the trail up the steep, stiff climb to the top of the headland. High up on the ridge once again, at one of

Opposite page: *Dark brown water tumbles into small plunge pools partially covered with aquatic vegetation.*
Above: *On the second day the trail crosses many appealing small streams.*

Left, above: *The characteristic brown colour of the Tsitsikamma water comes from the nutrients in the soil through which the water percolates.*
Below, left, right, and opposite page: *The Kleinbos River is one of the most beautiful rivers on the trail, a spot upstream providing a tranquil place for a meal and a swim.*

the highest points of the trail, a marvellous view of the coastline back to Skilderkrans is clearly visible.

The trail gently twists and dips down into the Geelhoutbos River gorge, and the second overnight spot, Scott. Where the Geelhoutbos River discharges its crystal brown water into the sea, the huts are tucked into the indigenous forest very close to the water's edge. The mouth of the river can offer a reasonable swimming spot when sea conditions allow. If you follow the right-hand fork of the river you will find a small pool tucked away among the rocks and trees. A lovely swimming spot, it also yields fresh water should the watertanks at the huts be dry.

Stiff muscles, scratched legs, sunburnt faces and aches and pains are forgotten as the evening shadows lengthen, friends huddle together around the fire against the chill of the night air, and the familiar smell of woodsmoke fills the air. As you climb into the comfort of a warm down sleeping bag the last thing you hear is the pounding of the surf.

Sunlight falls on the cold waters of the fern-hung Kleinbos River.

Top: *About 30 mm in diameter, this sea anemone is one of the many interesting and colourful organisms to be found in coastal rock pools.*

Above: *Where the Geelhoutbos River discharges its water into the sea, the huts at Scott are tucked into the indigenous vegetation close to the water's edge.*

Left: *One of the pleasures of the Trail is making time for a leisurely inspection of the inter-tidal scenery.*

Opposite page: *A magnificent bay of creamy beach, dark blue water and deep green forest, Blue Bay is a stunning detour on the trail.*

DAY THREE

7,7 km
(±4 hours)

Following a relatively even contour very close to the highwater mark the trail continues along the rocks towards the Elandsbos River. Along the trail there are numerous deep sheltered gullies where you will be rewarded on a plunge with a mask and snorkel into one of these pools.

The Elandsbos River is reached relatively early in the day, and is ideal for a relaxed tea break. The wide sandy river mouth is an excellent swimming spot for bodysurfing the salty waves, or you can pad across the creamy white sands of the river bed to plunge into the dark black depths of fresh water higher upstream.

Avoid the three false trails against the sand-dune on the far side of the river to minimise irreparable soil erosion. The real trail begins next to the large rocky outcrop about four hundred metres upstream.

After the Elandsbos River the trail becomes rugged, with frequent short inclines and declines that hug the coastline closely. The scenery of orange lichen-covered rocks, creamy beaches, deep green forest and turquoise sea is

stabbed with red aloes during the early winter months, which give a fiery contrast to the colours of the wild coastline.

Later in the day, after a relatively steep ascent to the top of the ridge, the bottom of the world drops away as Oakhurst appears on the opposite bank of the steep Lottering River gorge. The trail twists and winds down the sides of the gorge, diverting inland as the dark waters of the Lottering River appear. The river can be difficult to negotiate during high tides and heavy rains, and it is advisable to do a preliminary study of the tides.

The huts at Oakhurst, the third overnight spot, are a short distance from the point at which you cross the Lottering River.

Oakhurst possibly has the most dramatic setting of all the overnight spots. The huts are placed near each other in close proximity to the pounding waves. This is where you view the immense power of the sea in some spectacular displays of wave action during heavy seas. A small swell line changes tones from deep dark blue to bright turquoise as an almost even curl

Lined with forest and sand, the serene waters of the Elandsbos River create a scene of magnificent beauty and tranquillity.

33

of water reaches its summit and unleashes an eruption of bubbling, churning white water.

Among these blue lines of energy, streaks of silver-grey emerge into a sudden flash of white spray. One of nature's most beautiful creatures leaps in front of the wave with incredible speed and agility. The Indian Ocean Bottlenose Dolphin is renowned for its talent in the art of bodysurfing. These wonderful creatures are often encountered along the trail.

If Oakhurst's watertanks are dry, then water has to be drawn from the Lottering River. Water should be collected before high tide, as the sea pushes far upstream and makes the water salty.

The ranger stationed above Oakhurst is there to provide firewood and keep a check on the group size. He is in radio contact with the Park headquarters, so emergencies can be dealt with swiftly.

The Lottering River is a wonderful swimming spot, where the stiff, weary hiker can ease aches and pains by plunging into the crisp, cold water.

Above, left: *A young Cape clawless otter blinks in the sunlight.*
Above, right: *A fallen log links bands of colour in the Lottering River.*
Opposite page: *Mist rises from the Elandsbos River as it snakes its way silently to the sea.*

35

Right, top and bottom: *Oakhurst is
renowned for its magnificent seascapes,
often including wave-surfing dolphins –
a frequent sight along the trail.*
Opposite page: *Arguably the most
dramatic of all the overnight stops,
Oakhurst is positioned close to the sea.*

DAY FOUR

13,8 km
(±8 hours)

This day is reputed to be the most difficult day, mainly because of its length and the crossing of the legendary Bloukrans River.

From Oakhurst the trail follows the coastline very closely, dipping down to the rough rocks of the shore and rising up into patches of indigenous forest and open expanses of coastal fynbos. During the frequent declines the trail crosses small rivers. The Witels River is one of these rivers – an ideal spot for a short break, as fresh water is available in the river.

The trail beyond Witels River continues with regular short inclines and declines as the route goes westwards towards the Bloukrans River. Following a steady incline the trail climbs up to the ridge above and goes through patchy sections of fynbos, forest and crosses a few small streams. Collect fresh water at one of these small streams, as the Bloukrans River is salty and yields no fresh water supply.

Once out of the sparse forest, the trail slowly opens out into the Bloukrans River gorge, a river that has become legendary, branded as a major obstacle

on the trail. Under normal conditions the river is in fact the least of your worries and provides an excellent swimming spot with some wonderful bodysurfing. The Bloukrans River is an obvious teabreak spot, as André is still about three kilometres ahead.

The river crossing should be planned to co-ordinate with low tide. You should therefore make a preliminary check of the tide tables and plan the day accordingly. When it comes to crossing the river, it is expected that hikers use their initiative to plan the best route to the opposite bank. The structure of sandbanks in the mouth changes constantly, so no permanent route can be laid down. The easiest route is to cross directly to the largest cave on the landward side. From here you have the choice of going over the top along the footpath, or following the rocks above waterlevel to the point, where the trail starts again.

During heavy rains and large seas the river can be dangerous to negotiate. If these conditions should arise, an escape route on the eastern bank has been

Left and right: *The fourth day of the trail takes the hiker through coastal fynbos and indigenous forest on the way to Bloukrans River, climbing to headlands above stalwart cliffs and dropping to the coast again.*

Left and right: *Despite its reputation, the Bloukrans River is an easy crossing at low tide. Most hikers cross to the large cave on the opposite bank, and then walk along the rocks above the waterline to the point, where the trail continues.*

Above, left: *A common sight along the coast, rock hyrax, or dassies (Procavia capensis), bask in the early morning sunshine.*

Above, right: *A little way upstream, the Bloukrans River takes on the characteristic brown of Tsitsikamma water. Knysna lilies add a splash of colour to the foreground.*

provided. This very rough trail leads out to the national road. Once off the trail there is no return route back onto the opposite bank.

From the point of the western bank of the Bloukrans River the trail continues along the coastline tucked just into the forest above the highwater mark.

After winding up a short climb through the forest, the trail opens out onto an even ridge which follows the edge of a cliff-line above the rocky coast. The ridge is open and exposed, with coastal fynbos covering the gentle rolling gradient. This section of the trail offers some magnificent viewpoints of much of the coastline below.

The Klip River cuts a steep gorge through the ridge, and the last overnight point, André, is tucked away in this valley. From the pile of wood stacked for hikers up on the ridge the trail twists down through the forest to the two huts. The ranger based near the woodpile above André is there to keep check on hikers and ensure that all is well. Any emergencies can also be dealt with.

André is tucked away among the low coastal forest vegetation close to smooth pebble beaches at the mouth of the Klip River. This river is well established and provides an ideal swimming spot a short distance upstream. Plunging into the crisp water after a long day's hike will provoke gasps of delight.

At dusk the candlelit atmosphere of the huts and the drifting smell of woodsmoke provide the familiar smell of a hiking trail.

On this, the last night of the trail, a sense of close comradeship draws everyone together around the fire – reluctant to leave the group, the trail and the sense of freedom. Happiness, contentment and a feeling of achievement linger as the last red coals of the fire die down later than usual.

Above, left and right: *The huts at André, the last overnight stop, are a welcome sight after the longest day's hike.*

DAY FIVE

6,8 km
(±3 hours)

From André the trail begins on the opposite bank of the Klip River and climbs very steeply to the top of the ridge above the valley. Once on the ridge the trail continues on an even contour along the edge of the cliffs towards Nature's Valley. Here you go through open expanses of coastal fynbos, then drop down into a steep gorge through which the Helpmekaar River flows.

The trail climbs out of the Helpmekaar River gorge and continues along the ridge. Eventually Nature's Valley opens out, with its beautiful creamy white beach. The trail drops down steeply, winding through the rugged mountainside and eventually leads out onto the beach. Here, trudging across the soft white sand, you come to the end of the trail at the Groot River, the official boundary of the Tsitsikamma Coastal National Park. A ranger is stationed close to the river and is usually to be found patrolling the beach.

Driving up the pass from Nature's Valley you now feel recharged and well-prepared for the battles that face you in everyday life. It is a feeling so good . . . that it feels as though you have just swallowed sunshine.

Opposite page and below right: *On the last day the trail goes along the tops of towering cliffs, providing a magnificent view back along the trail.* Right, above: *A beautiful member of the Amaryllidaceae family, the Knysna or George Lily* (Cyrtanthus purpureus) *flowers from December to February and is a common sight along the trail.*

45

The end of the trail, Nature's Valley, offers an inviting sweep of sand and sea for a last swim.

The last part of the Otter Trail – the beach at Nature's Valley – offers soft white sand for weary feet.

USEFUL INFORMATION

Because of its popularity, the Otter Trail has to be managed under strict control. For this reason hikers have to book for the trail, and no more than 12 people, or two parties of six, may leave each day. Bookings for the trail can be made at the two National Parks Board regional offices in Cape Town and Pretoria. No bookings for the trail are accepted at the Tsitsikamma National Park headquarters at Storms River Mouth. Enquiries and information are, however, obtainable at the Park headquarters. A brochure containing a map and the rules and regulations, as well as information on the flora and fauna, is supplied with each booking.

Such is the popularity of the Otter Trail that bookings often have to be made up to one year in advance. Hikers desperately seeking a booking should enquire frequently at the offices, as cancellations are sometimes received. Tariff increases must be paid in addition to the permit fees for the trail when the permit for the trail is collected at the Park.

Bookings for accommodation facilities at the Park restcamp can be made at the regional offices in Cape Town and Pretoria. Entrance fees and overnight tariffs are amended in April each year: people who intend visiting the Park are advised to make preliminary enquiries about the fees and tariffs involved, and to acquaint themselves with the rules and regulations.

National Parks Board regional offices
Pretoria: P O Box 787, Pretoria, 0001 Tel. (012) 343-1991
Cape Town: P O Box 7400, Roggebaai, 8012 Tel. (021) 22-2810

Information about the Park can be obtained from the two regional offices or at the Tsitsikamma Coastal National Park, P O Storms River, 6308 Tel. (04237) 651/2/3.

ACKNOWLEDGEMENTS

My special thanks go to the following people and organisations (not in order of preference): Bridget Dilkes; Peter Slingsby; Elizabeth Marshall; John Allen; Johan Kloppers; the Psalm 91 Hiking Party; Creative Colour Photographic laboratory; the National Parks Board – especially the staff of the Tsitsikamma Coastal National Park, who were always so warm and friendly; Professor Eugene Moll and Peta Masson of the Botany Department, University of Cape Town; and Pieter Struik and Kate McCallum for their flawless advice.

Acknowledgements are also due to the following photographers who gave permission for their photographs to be used in this book:

Anthony Bannister (cover photograph, Knysna loerie on p. 13, Gazania daisies and lichen on p. 16, Sea anemone and inter-tidal scene p. 31, Cape clawless otter on p. 35, trail landscape on p. 38);
Johan Hosten (hiker on p. 1, hikers on p. 48);
Peter Steyn (Black oystercatcher on p. 9);
Johan van Papendorp (hikers climbing cliff on p. 39, hiker cooking on p. 43);
Map: Etienne van Duyker.